Picnic Walks with Children around Derby and Derbyshire

Written and illustrated

by Hazel Glover

April 2021

Picnic Walks for Children around Derby and Derbyshire

Acknowledgements

Thank you to the National Stone Centre for their kind permission to include their Geotrail in the book.

Thank you also to my family and friends for their assistance in compiling and testing these routes: my partner Mike for helping with research; and our grandchildren Jemima, Heidi, Sonja, Saga and Edward with their parents Kerry and Dan, Matthew and Linn, Holly and Paul, who helped to test the walks.

Picnic Walks for Children around Derby and Derbyshire

INTRODUCTION

These walks are designed for families with children, depending on their abilities. Those able to read may lead the way.

Each walk gives ideas for activities and suggests useful items to take along. The walks are varying lengths so that there is something for even the toddlers. The walks get progressively longer and harder through the book. Many include a playground and picnic facilities, and some have café and toilets available.

Suggestions for parking are provided and there is information about the type of terrain. **These are countryside walks so young children must be supervised at all times, especially around water and animals**, and the writer takes no responsibility for any accidents or damage.

Country paths will often be muddy and slippery in wet weather, so please take extra care in these situations. Boundaries and landmarks can change over time.

Please follow the Countryside Code:

Respect other people

- Consider the local people and others enjoying the outdoors
- Park carefully so access to gateways and driveways is clear
- Leave gates and property as you find them
- Follow paths but give way to others where it's narrow.

Protect the Natural Environment

- Leave no trace of your visit, take all your litter home
- Don't have BBQs or fires
- Keep dogs under effective control
- Dog poo - bag it and bin it

Enjoy the outdoors

- Plan ahead, check what facilities are open, be prepared
- Follow advice and local signs and obey social distancing measures

[Source: Gov.uk]

Picnic Walks for Children around Derby and Derbyshire

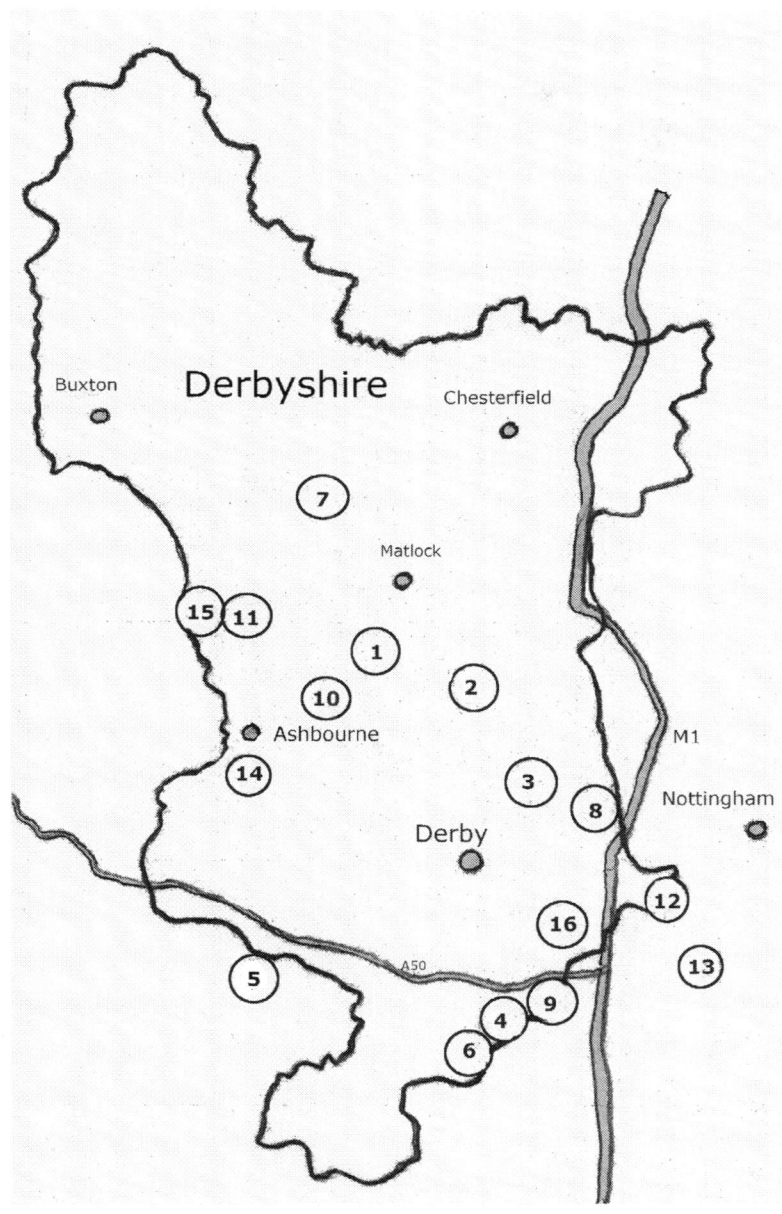

Contents

		Page
1.	High Peak Trail and National Stone Centre – 1 mile	11
2.	Woodland adventure in Whatstandwell – 1.5 miles (dog friendly)	16
3.	Dale Abbey and the Hermit's Cave – 1.7 miles	21
4.	Ticknall to Staunton Harold Reservoir – 1.8 miles (adaptable for pushchair)	27
5.	Tutbury Mill Fleam Walk – 1.9 miles	31
6.	Dimminsdale to Staunton Harold Hall – 2.3 miles	37
7.	Stanton Moor and the Nine Ladies Circle – 2.4 miles (dog friendly)	43
8.	Straw's Bridge and the Nutbrook Trail – 2.5 miles (Escape route reduces to 1.5 miles)	48

		Page
9.	Swarkestone Pavilion Walk – 2.6 miles (Escape Route reduces to 1.9 miles)	54
10.	Carsington Reservoir - 2.6 miles (Pushchair, cycle and dog friendly)	60
11.	Tissington - 2.7 miles (Escape Route reduces to 1 mile)	65
12.	Long Eaton and Attenborough – 3.3 miles (Pushchair, cycle and dog friendly)	72
13.	Sutton Bonington and the Zouch Cut – 4.3 miles (Escape Route reduces to 2.8 miles)	78
14.	Snelston and the River Dove – 4.4 miles	86
15.	Thorpe, Mapleton and the River Dove – 4.4 miles	94
16.	Shardlow and Church Wilne – 4.6 miles (Escape Routes reduce to 0.5 miles, 3.2 miles and 4 miles).	102

1. High Peak Trail and National Stone Museum

Distance: 1 mile

Description: A marked route with rocky tracks and paths around quarries, showing how the rocks were formed. My grandchildren (2-6 yrs) enjoyed climbing on rocks, discovering fossils, climbing on stiles, building stones and a picnic next to the playground.

Facilities: Fossil hunting, fossil wax rubbing, rock clambering, stone walling, playground, toilets, Discovery Centre.

Parking: Car park signposted for Eco Discovery, National Stone Museum and Blue Lagoon approximately ½ mile along Porter Lane (DE4 4LS) on the Cromford to Wirksworth Road, B5036 (parking charge applies). Car park is right at the end of the lane after an adventure playground on the left. Google Link 3CVG+CH Matlock

Useful items: Wax crayons and paper, picnic, walking shoes.

Picnic Walks for Children around Derby and Derbyshire

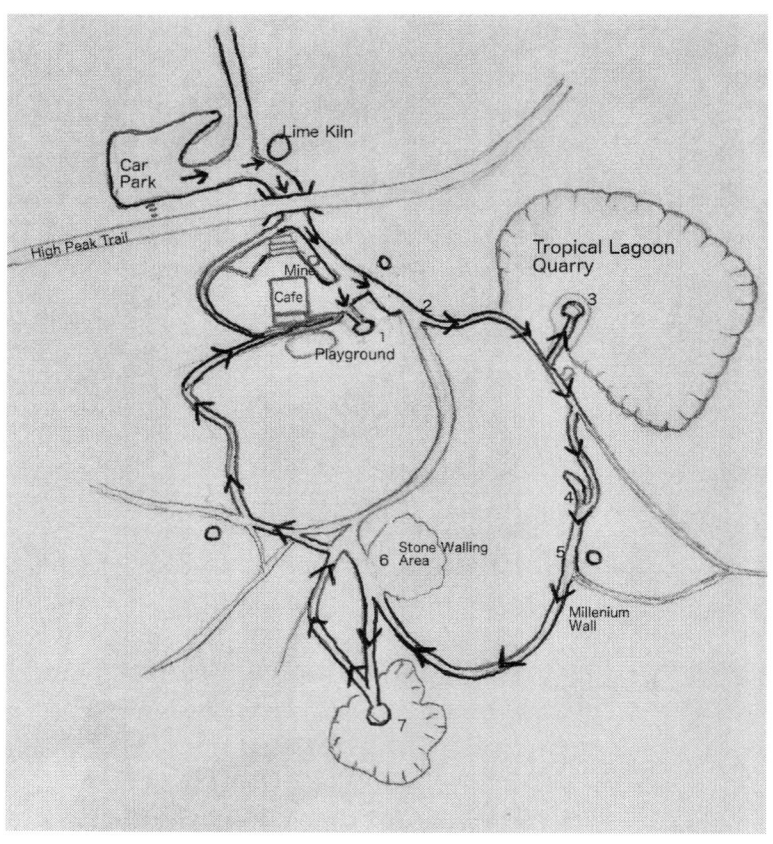

1. From the payment machine at the carpark, go towards the bridge archway and look for the lime kiln on the left just before the bridge.

A lime kiln was used to produce Quicklime from limestone rocks. Quicklime is used to make cement and plaster.

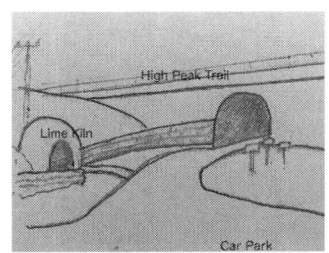

Question: **Where did the workers put the limestone?**
Answer: **In the top of the kiln**

2. Go under the bridge and walk down the slope towards the café. Look out for the old lead mine tunnel on the right.

3. In front of the Discovery Centre, look for a rock with a red flower painted on top (sometimes hidden by parked cars). Go up behind it to find the Number One marker post and the first fossil rubbing.

4. Returning to the large rock, turn right towards the tower where children can clamber up over the rocks. Find the Number Two marker post which reveals the second fossil image.

Question: **What is the name of the fossil?**
Answer: **Solitary Coral**

5. Close by, a signpost points the way to the Eco Trail. Follow the path on the left and find marker Number Three at the quarry look-out point. Can you imagine that this area was once a Tropical Lagoon?

6.   Back on the main track, ignore the footpath to the left and fork right to find marker Number Four in a dip on the right. Another fossil rubbing can be made here.

> *In front of the marker to the left is an outcrop of rock. If you look carefully you will find more fossils, similar to the one on the marker.*

7.   Back on the main track, head upwards towards an obelisk and the Millenium Wall plaque. There is another fossil rubbing close by.

> *These walls are examples of stone-walling which is common around fields in Derbyshire.*

8.   Follow the stone wall circle round to find marker Number Six.

Activity: Can you build a stone wall with the limestone rocks?

9.   Go back to the path and turn sharply left round a circular wall to find marker Number Seven and another fossil on the edge of a large quarry. Can you see the layers of the rock which can reveal the types of creatures which lived millions of years ago?

10.   Follow the path around and head towards another stone tower. At the footpath sign keep to the right of the tower going up a zigzag path to the playground, where you can have a picnic on the rocks or try activities and refreshments in the Discovery Centre.

11.   Up the slope to the bridge will take you back to the carpark on the left.

2. Woodland Adventure in Whatstandwell (Dog friendly)

Distance: 1.5 miles

Description: Rocky tracks and paths. **There are a couple of tricky slopes which may be slippy in wet weather** and a walking stick is recommended.

Facilities: Rock clambering, feeding ducks, quarry. Refreshments available at the Family Tree.

Parking: Car park by the canal bridge in Whatstandwell (DE4 5HG) just before the Holloway turn. Space is limited but there is alternative parking on the roadside or down a lane on the A6 bend by the Family Tree. Google Link 3FPV+4W Matlock

Useful items: Duck food, walking stick, walking shoes, picnic if required.

Picnic Walks for Children around Derby and Derbyshire

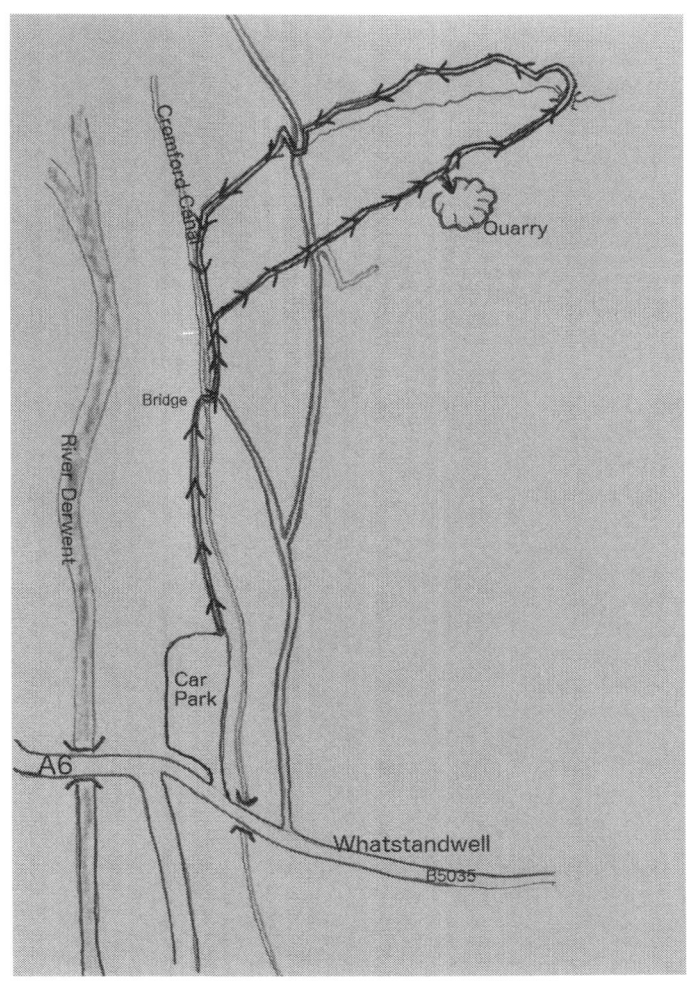

1. From the car park on the canal side, turn left along the towpath and walk a quarter of a mile to a bridge across the canal. Just before the bridge, take the left fork up a slip road to cross the bridge over the canal.

There may be some ducks along the canal. They will come to you if you give them some duck food.

2. As you enter the wood, take the left path, following a well-worn route which bends right to leave the canal.

The ruins of a building alongside this path were part of Sims Wharf which was used to load sandstone and gritstone from the quarries in the woods. It is believed that this building was the stables.

3. Ignoring smaller paths on the left, continue along the path which slopes gently uphill to a gateway and then carefully cross the road to continue the path on the other side.

Question: **Some trees have silver bark – what are they called?**
Answer: **Silver Birch**

4. Follow the sign for Wakebridge, taking the left fork and ignore the path on the right. Follow this gently uphill through the wood until you reach a fallen tree across the path. Limbo under the tree. [In case the tree has been removed, keep a look out for the quarry entrance on the right.]

5. The quarry on the right is often used by climbers. This could be a picnic spot, and there are further quarries nearby. After exploring the quarries, return to the main path.

6. Continue along this main path until you reach a stream crossed by a wooden bridge. Immediately after this, turn left, ignoring the stile in the wall. Continue into woodland with the stone wall on your right. **This path may be slippy and tricky in wet weather, so please take care.**

There are holly bushes along this path. Can you spot one?

7. Carry on along this path which follows the route of the stream on your left until you reach a road.

Can you spot Crich Stand on the far hills?

8.   Cross the road and turn left over the road bridge – TAKE CARE, BUSY ROAD. Turn sharply right down a track which says RESIDENTS PARKING ONLY. Follow the road around a bend.

> *The house ahead looks very small, but as you pass it down the slope, look back to see how big the house really is!*

9.   Just before the house, there is a wooden bridge across the stream. Cross the bridge and turn right following the path along the stream.

10.   As you reach the canal, continue on the path with the canal on your right.

11.   Continue alongside the canal until you reach the wooden bridge where you crossed earlier. Cross the bridge and turn left to return along the canal path to the car park.

3. Dale Abbey and the Hermit's Cave

Distance: 1.7 miles

Description: This is an easy walk through woodland and fields.

Facilities: The walk includes a Hermit's Cave, monastery ruins, a playground and the Carpenters Arms is en route for refreshments

Parking: A layby on Potato Pit Lane, Dale Abbey opposite Dale Road, DE7 4PH. Google Link WMR5+P8 Ilkeston

Useful items: Picnic.

Picnic Walks for Children around Derby and Derbyshire

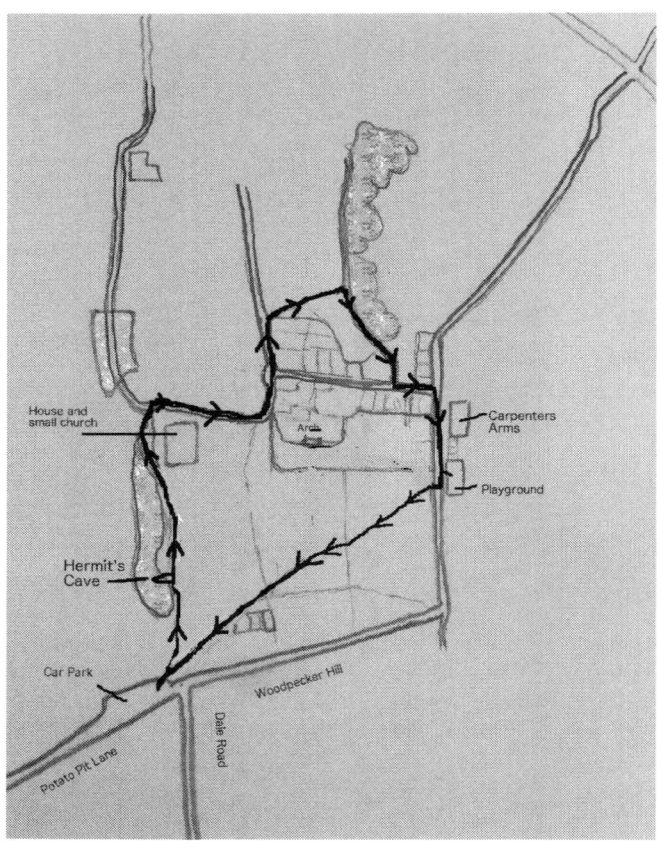

1.   Facing the road in the layby, turn left to find a footpath sign and gateway into a field. In the field, go slightly right over a mound to reach the corner of a wood. Ignore the path which goes diagonally across the field, and keep close to the boundary on your left.

22

In the distance slightly to the right, you can see the arch of the former monastery. Further to the right, there is a windmill visible on the horizon.

2. Follow the edge of the wood with the boundary on your left and go through a gate with plaques for Hermit's Wood.

According to records, the hermit was a Derby baker called Cornelius who was sent to Dale Abbey by a dream of the Virgin Mary in the 12th Century.

3. Ignore the flight of steps on your left and go further to another flight of steps. Go up these steps to visit the hermit's cave, descending by the steps on the other side, taking care not to slip on the slopes.

4. As you return to the main path, turn left and continue until there is a fork in the path. Take the left fork up the slope, coming down to a track beside a house. Turn right.

5. Head towards the white gate at the side of the cemetery and look back towards the house to see the tiny church in the side.

This house has the tiny church of All Saints tucked in the side and was once part of the infirmary for the monastery which was built on the site shortly after the death of the hermit. The house later became the Bluebell Inn, and is now a private house.

6. Continue along the track and just before the bend, there is a footpath sign on the right by a small gate. If you would like a close-up view of the monastery arch, take this footpath, hugging the fence as it bends to the left to reach the arch. Return on the same path to continue the walk.

The monastery was destroyed on the orders of Henry VIII in 1538, when he disbanded all monasteries and confiscated their funds.

7. Around the bend there is a junction with seats and a tree in the centre. At this junction take the left fork (Tattle Hill) and walk a short distance to a footpath on the right in the corner of a field. There is a stile but an easier route is a slight slope at the side.

Just before the junction, there are some houses that have been built with the stones from the monastery.

This house has been built around part of the old building. Can you see which part?

8.   Keep to the hedge on your right, to find a gap in the holly at the corner and go over the stile to reach a wider track. Turn right on this track.

9.   This track goes over a stile and along the back of properties until you appear to be going into a garden. Turn sharp left here along a beech hedge to emerge in front of garages.

> *On your right as you near the road are the remains of the Abbey Gatehouse, which was once used for prisoners in transit to Derby.*

10.   Walk to the road in front of Abbey Cottage and turn left to reach the corner opposite the Carpenter's Arms. Carefully cross the main road (Arbour Hill) and turn right along the pavement.

11.   On this road you will pass an old phone box and shortly afterwards, beside the old school, there is a play area on the left with seats that could be a good picnic spot.

12. After leaving the play area, turn left and continue past the 30 mph sign to reach a footpath sign on the right, just past a field gate. Cross the road and go over the stile into the field.

13. The path goes diagonally left across the field to a stile in the centre of the boundary opposite. In the next field the path keeps diagonally left past a tree beside a marshy area to reach an open gateway in the left corner of the boundary.

14. Keeping left, go straight ahead past a large fallen tree to reach the stile which brings you back to the layby.

4. Ticknall to Staunton Harold Reservoir (adaptable for pushchair)

Distance: 1.8 miles

Description: An easy walk along a reservoir with a picnic spot and playground midway. The first half is pushchair friendly. There is also woodland to explore and a small beach.

Facilities: Playground, café, toilets, beach, ducks to feed.

Parking: Broadstone Lane, Ticknall (DE73 7JT). There are two areas to park; either is okay if you are doing the full walk. The first is a lay-by on the left by a footpath sign (4 spaces) and the second is 100 yards further in a turning point by another footpath (4 spaces). Google Link RG6W+75 Derby

Useful items: Duck food, picnic.

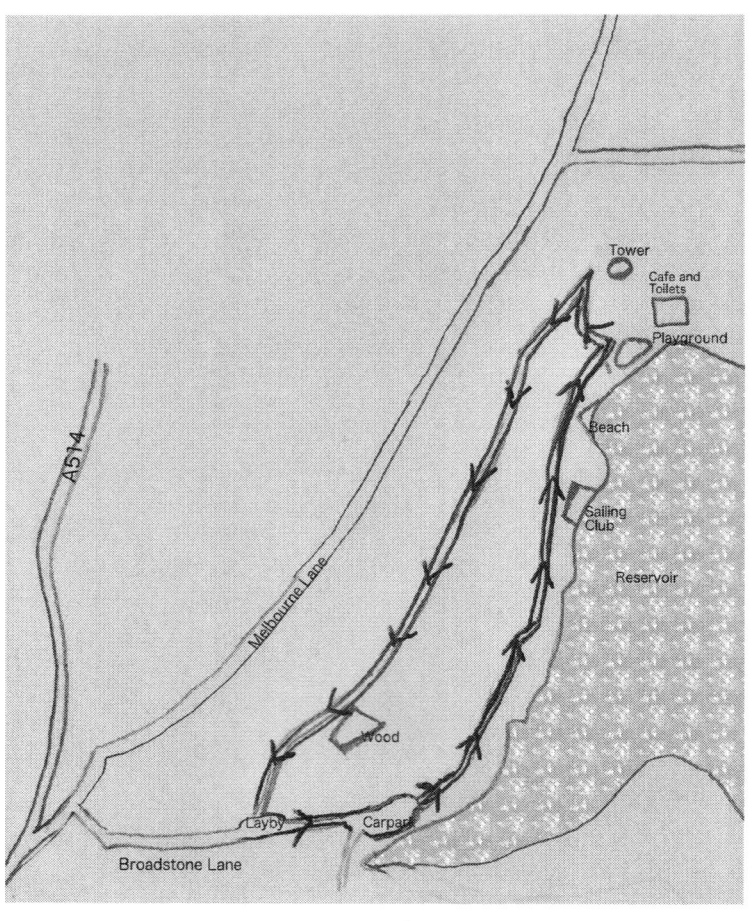

1. From the turning point, take the tarmac footpath alongside the reservoir until you reach the sailing club. There are alternate rough footpaths closer to the reservoir if you prefer.

Question: **What animal makes the earth mounds in the fields?**
Answer: **Moles**

2.   A short way after the Sailing Club, follow the footpath sign to the right to reach the beach. This is usually a good place to feed the ducks.

3.   Continue along the side of the reservoir to reach the picnic and play area, where you can also find the café and toilets.

[For pushchair route, return by retracing your steps.]

4.   For the full walk, go alongside the car park up to the watchtower keeping the hedge on your left. Find a footpath in the hedge on the left just after the road turns right.

5.   Turning diagonally left in this field, follow the telegraph poles until they run out. Keep in the same direction to reach Derby Hills wood. Explore the wood if you wish and return to the path.

6.   Keeping the wood on your left go to a stile in the corner going slightly right. Follow the fenced path to reach a stile into a paddock.

7.   Keep the hedge on your left to another stile into a grazing field. Cross slightly left to another stile and then keep in the same direction to a kissing gate in the left corner, bringing you out on the road at the lay-by. Turn left if you parked in the turning point.

5. Tutbury Mill Fleam Walk

Distance: 1.9 miles

Description: An easy walk from Tutbury Mill picnic ground along the Mill Fleam and around Tutbury Castle ruins. It is mainly field paths with stiles and a weir bridge. **PLEASE KEEP CHILDREN SAFE BY WATER.**

Facilities: Playground, picnic area, cafés and shops nearby. Tutbury Castle and the café have published opening hours at tutburycastle.com.

Parking: Tutbury Mill Picnic Site, Bridge Street/A511, Tutbury DE13 9LZ. Google Ref V868+GG Burton-on-Trent.

Useful items: Picnic.

Picnic Walks for Children around Derby and Derbyshire

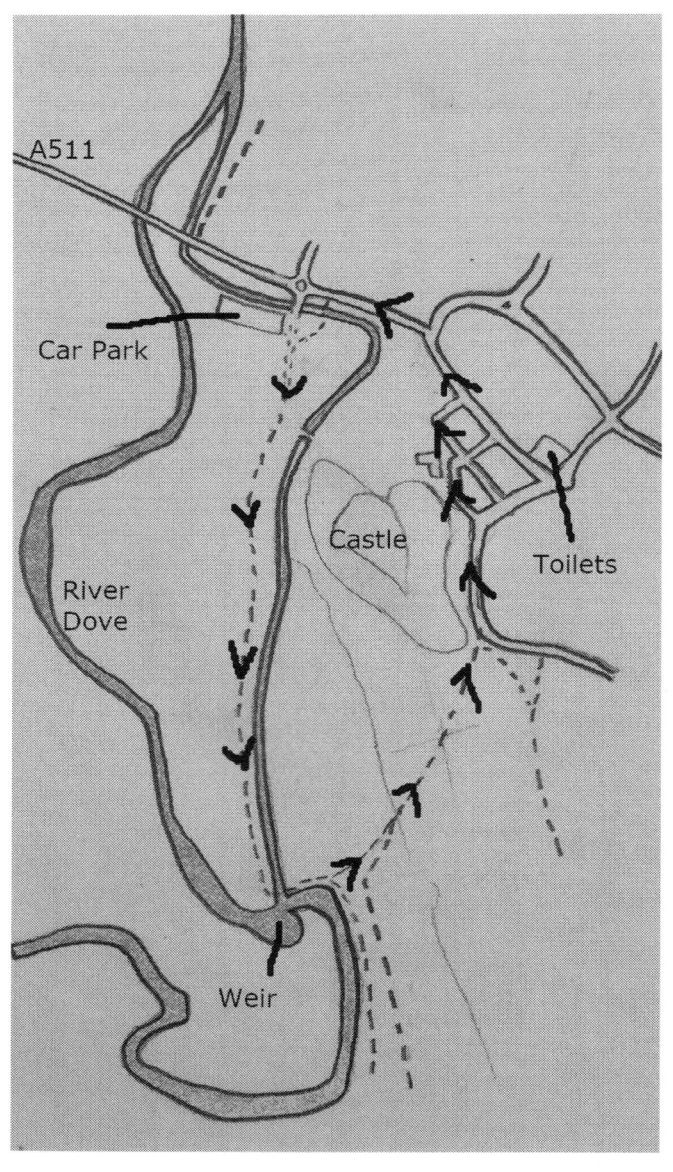

1. From the car park, walk back to the access track and turn right towards the cricket ground. Go through a kissing gate beside a gate at the side of the Cricket Club, marked Private Fishing.

2. Continue along the track, keeping the same direction when the hard surface disappears into the grass. Head for a flat bridge over the stream.

3. Veer left following the stream until it disappears under the field. Keep in the same direction walking parallel with the boundary on your left.

> *The Mill Fleam used to power the old Cornmill, and later a cotton mill. The fields around the Castle were formerly the Deer Park.*

4. Continue along this fence until you reach the weir. **PLEASE KEEP CHILDREN SAFE BY THE WEIR.**

5. Turn left in front of the weir to go through a gate and over a bridge.

6. Follow the river round to the right to the bend and then head across the middle of the field towards the line of houses on the horizon. There is a stile in the middle of the hedge line, and this takes you over a wooden bridge into another field. You can see the castle on the hill to the left.

The medieval Tutbury Castle dates back to the 14th Century when it was home to Henry de Ferrers. By 1370, it had passed to John of Gaunt. Mary Queen of Scots was imprisoned here in 1568. [Source: Tutburycastle.com]

7. Go diagonally left across the field to the corner, and over the broken stile in the corner. Then immediately turn right to go through an ungated gateway.

Picnic Walks for Children around Derby and Derbyshire

8. Turn sharply left towards a path on the right side of the castle and to the left of the houses. This path goes quite steeply up to a kissing gate and a series of steps. Continue along this path as it goes between the houses and then turn left on to the road.

9. Keep left as the pavement forks to go in front of Castle Hill House and then turn left on the road up towards the castle. Ignore the entrance gate in front and turn sharp right by the graveyard to go into the churchyard.

Activity: Can you find the stocks beside the church. What were they used for?

Answer: These were used as a form of punishment to humiliate offenders.

10. Keeping the church on your left, continue straight on through the churchyard, ignoring paths to the left and right, to reach a gate into an alley with railings on the right-hand side.

11. At the end of the alley, go straight on along the drive to a roadway where you turn left. Keep to the left along this road.

> *There are several cafés and shops in this area, particularly through Tutbury Mill Mews.*

12. Keep on the left along Bridge Street, until just before the road sign for the roundabout there is a footpath access on the left which leads into the picnic site. The car park is ahead.

Tutbury Castle, North Tower

6. Dimminsdale and Staunton Harold Craft Centre

Distance: 2.3 miles

Description: Rocky tracks and paths. Sheep and cows in surrounding fields. There is a short steep slope at the beginning, but then it is fairly easy walking. Dimminsdale is a nature reserve which has interesting walkways and wooden bridges, as well as a lime kiln.

Facilities: Woodland, feeding ducks, stiles with poetry, games, café, toilets and shops in the Ferrers Craft Centre. There is also a Garden Centre with another café.

Parking: Car park at the Dimminsdale Picnic Spot by the reservoir. It is accessed from the A587 from Melbourne, with a right turn signposted by a brown anvil. (DE73 8BJ) Google Link 9C4WQHV6+G4 Derby

Useful items: Duck food, walking stick, walking shoes, picnic if required.

Picnic Walks for Children around Derby and Derbyshire

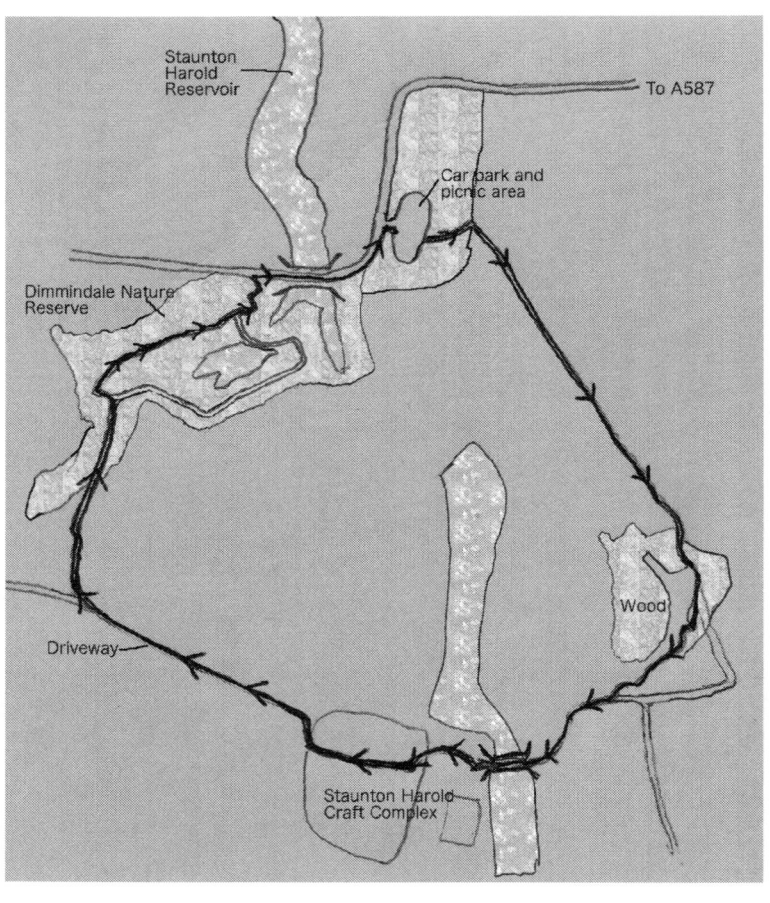

1. From the entrance to the car park, look slightly right beyond the parked cars. To the left of a picnic table, take the flight of steps going up into the trees. Can you find any acorns in this wood?

Question: What trees do acorns come from?

Answer: Oak trees

2. At the top of the climb, go through the stile into a field.

> *Can you read the words on the stile? These words are part of a poem which is revealed completely in a longer walk. One poem reads forward and the words on the reverse side of the stiles are from another poem.*

3. Turn right and continue through two fields to reach another stile into a wood. The poem continues on this stile.

4. Follow the path through the wood until you reach a driveway. Turn left on this driveway and then immediately right to follow a wide path into the wood. This path twists and turns and then starts to go downwards, to emerge through another stile into a field. The date and initials on this stile relate to the author of the poem, John Blunt.

5. Continue slightly right around the wall, heading towards Staunton Harold Hall, which can be seen in the distance. A yellow marker shows the way. Leave the field via a small gate and turn right on the drive.

6. Go through the gateway and continue across the bridge and along the drive to reach a car park on the other side of the hall. There are seats at the side of the lake which could be a picnic spot with an opportunity to feed the ducks in the lake.

Question: **What creatures can you see on top of the gateposts?**

Answer: **A stag and a dog**

7. Following the driveway, go around the car park which curves to the left. You may be able to see statues in the grounds of the Hall as you reach the corner.

8. Follow the drive round to the right between the buildings. There is an opportunity here to try out the shops and the café in the Ferrers Centre on the right, where there is  also a garden chess game available at times. There is a Garden Centre and Café further along the road on the left and toilets are available behind the Stable Yard Café.

> *Around the courtyard, you can see swallows' nests in the corners of the top windows. In the spring you may be lucky enough to see the swallows flying to these nests to feed the young.*

9. After exploring the Craft Centre, return to the driveway and follow this past the garden centre, over a cattle grid and straight on down the hill. Watch for cars along this drive. There may be animals grazing along the way.

10. As the hedge and fence on the right comes to an end, turn sharp right into the field to follow the footpath sign to Harpur's Hill, keeping the boundary on your right. At the end of the field, the path continues through a wooded area and through a gate signed for Ivanhoe Way. A little further along this path brings you to a stile and plaque for Dimminsdale.

This area used to be quarried by a small community which produced quicklime in a lime kiln in the eastern end of the reserve. There is a circular path around the reserve which was made clockwise during the Covid outbreak.

11. As you enter Dimminsdale, turn left along the circular path which curves slightly right. When you reach the bottom of the lake, there is a flight of steps on the left and two wooden bridges over a stream on the right. Turn left up the steps.

12. Continue across the walkways to reach the road. Turn right to cross the bridge over the reservoir and you will reach a stile leading to the car park.

This is the full poem if you do the 6 mile walk. Can you recognize what the poem is describing?

*Our paired legs stand
To let your paired legs pass
Give us your hand
We'll lead you where
The grass is greener yet.*

John Blunt 1994

7. Stanton Moor and the Nine Ladies Circle (Dog friendly)

Distance: 2.4 miles

Description: This is an easy moorland walk with unusual rocks, Grey's tower, a trig point and an early Bronze Age stone circle.

Facilities: Rock clambering, woodland tracks.

Parking: Car park on Birchover Road opposite Birchover Stone Limited DE4 2BN. Google Link 5955+JQ Matlock

Useful items: Walking stick, picnic if required.

Picnic Walks for Children around Derby and Derbyshire

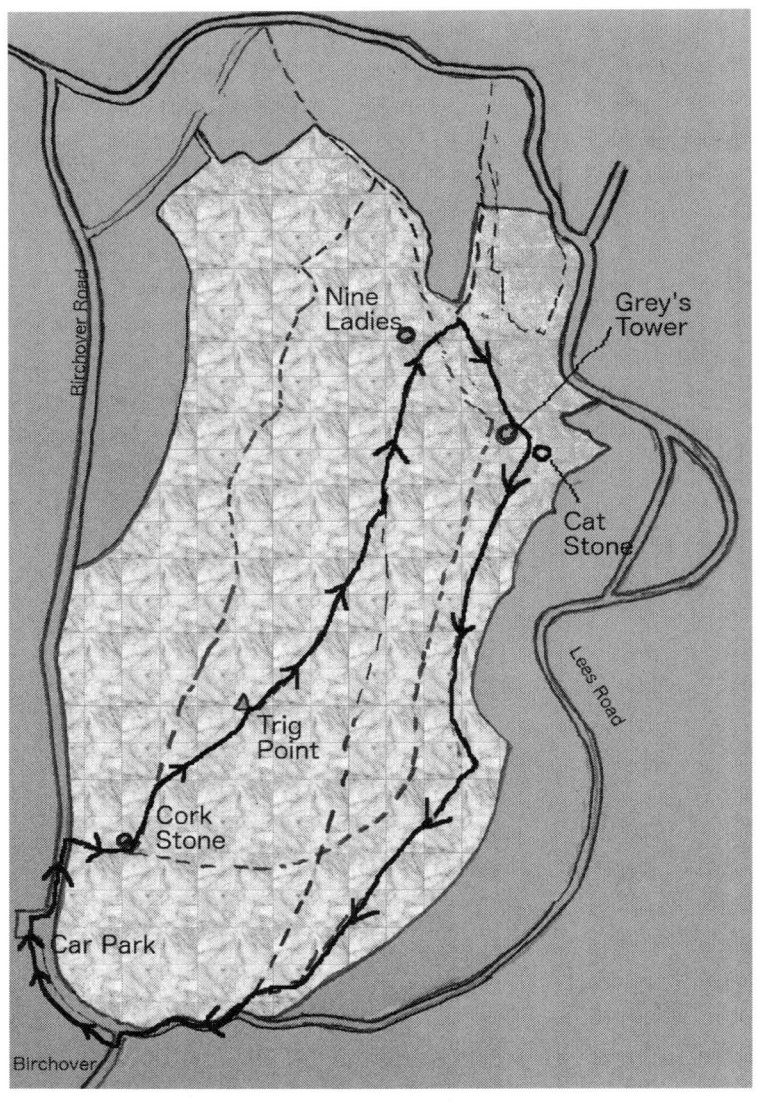

1. From the car park, turn left along the road for a quarter of a mile until you see a footpath sign on the opposite side of the road, beside a long square slab of stone. Ignore the unmarked path into a quarry – the footpath is a little further along the road.

2. Follow the footpath through a gate and around the bottom of a slope until you see the Cork Stone in front of you, with climbing holds attached.

3. From the Cork Stone, take the left fork alongside a quarry, but after a short distance take a narrow grassy path on the right, almost opposite the quarry. This path leads you to a trig point, with views across Derbyshire.

A trig point, or Triangulation Point, was used as a navigational aid for surveying the positions of roads etc. [Source: Wikipedia]

4. Continue along the path for around half a mile to reach a T-junction with a wider path. Turn left on this path for approximately a third of a mile until you reach the open space with the Nine Ladies stones. There is a plaque which gives information about them.

This is a good picnic stop. It is believed that this was a central point for a Bronze Age settlement.

5. In front of the plaque there is a wide path going off to the right of the main path. Ignore this and walk on for around 25 metres to find a narrow path on the right going through the trees. This leads to a stile in a fence ahead. Go over the stile and turn right along a narrow path – watch out for trip hazards!

6. Follow this path for about a quarter of a mile until you reach Grey's Tower.

This tower was built in honour of Charles, the second Earl Grey, who was Prime Minister in 1830 and introduced the 1832 Reform Bill which gave every man the right to vote. His government

also brought about the abolition of slavery in 1833.
[Source: Wikipedia]

7.   Continue along the path until you reach the Cat Stone. Do you think it looks like a cat?

8.   After exploring the Stone, return to the main path to continue around the bend. This path follows the boundary of Stanton Moor for around three quarters of a mile, passing a sign for Stanton Moor Edge by another large boulder, which you may wish to explore. Ignore any other paths until you reach the road.

9.   Turn right along the road, walking to the junction. Go left slightly past the junction and cross the road to a gate and a footpath through the wall on the right. This path goes through a field of mini stone cairns to reach the car park.

Activity: Can you build a stone cairn?

8. Straw's Bridge and the Nutbrook Trail

Distance: 2.5 miles (Escape route reduces to 1.5 miles)

Description: This walk is fairly easy around woodland, lakes and a nature reserve. There are some rough paths through woodland and fields, with stiles and kissing gates.

Facilities: Picnic tables, bird sanctuary

Parking: Car park at Straw's Bridge on the A609 between Ilkeston and West Hallam, DE7 5FG. Google Link XM8C+WX Ilkeston

Useful items: Duck food, bird identifier, binoculars, picnic if required.

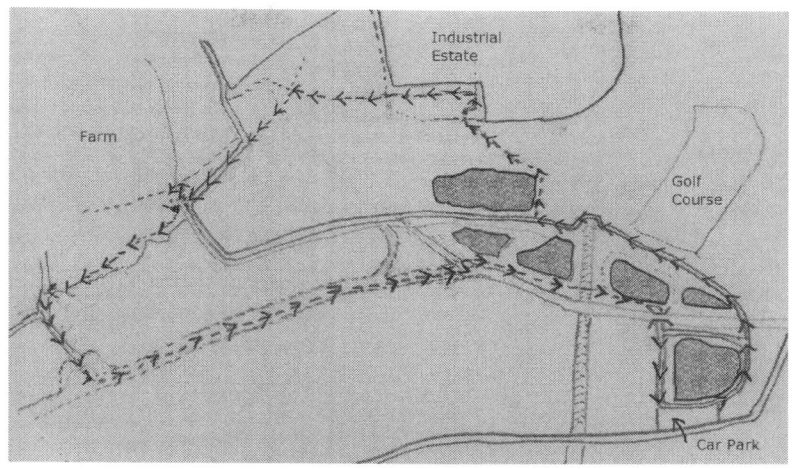

1. From the car park, go anti-clockwise around the lake, passing the entrance and the picnic tables.

Straw's Bridge is on the site of former open cast mines and the old Nutbrook canal. It gets its name from a former canal bridge over the Nutbrook Canal for the road now known as the A609. In 1844 Samuel Straw

was an overseer for the canal and he was paid 18 shillings a week with a house rent-free. [Source: friendsofstrawsbridge.co.uk]

Activity: How many swans can you see on the lake? Can you spot a tufted duck? (Black and white with a feather tuft on its head, as shown.)

2.   At the far corner of the lake, take the right fork up the slope and away from the lake, signposted Cycle Track Route 67. Turn left at the gate at the top of the rise, and left again on to the Nutbrook trail.

3.   Continue on the tarmac path with the stream on your left until you see a bridge over the stream where the path swings to the right. You can follow the track around the mound, or take the shortcut over the top, to reach the Manor Floods Nature Reserve.

4.   Follow the path with a lake on your left. As the lake on the left disappears, another appears on the right. Turn right just before this lake to go anticlockwise around it.

5.   As you reach the far side, there are several tracks leaving the lake and going up the slope. Take one of these and follow the line of the telegraph poles

diagonally left, until you see a line of grey railings in the far boundary. Head towards these railings and go through the gateway beside them.

6. Follow this tarmac track as it curves right then left. There is a copse and a kissing gate on the left just after the bend, marked Circular Route 6. Go through the gate and follow the path uphill through the trees.

7. The path roughly follows the boundary of the industrial estate and then descends into open grassland. Turn immediately sharp right to continue along the path following the boundary.

8. The path forks as the fence on the right comes to an end. Keep to the left fork to continue through the woodland until you meet a wider path crossing from left to right. Turn left on to the wider path.

Activity: Look out for signs of horses, as this is a bridle path. You may be able to spot hoofprints.

9. This path meets a tarmac path on a bend with a seat opposite. Turn left on the tarmac path and walk to the next sharp left hand bend. [This point is an Escape Route. If you wish to cut the walk by 1 mile, then follow the tarmac path left back to the start.]

10.   To complete the full walk, DO NOT GO ROUND THE BEND. Go straight ahead into the copse and turn immediately right on a rough path to go over a stile into farmland.

11.   Turn left on to a plank bridge between the fields, and then immediately left again to follow the boundary of the field on the left. Keep following the boundary round 2 sides of the field, sometimes with a brook on the left, until you reach a gate in the far corner. Go over the stile beside the gate, and keep left, towards a gateway with a kissing gate. Go through the kissing gate into a wide area which often has piles of gravel around. Go through this area to reach the wide path which was a former railway track. Turn left on to this track.

12.   When the tarmac track bends sharp left under a line of telegraph wires, leave the path and go straight ahead on to a rough path into the trees, keeping the fence on your right. Ignore kissing gates on your right and keep in the same direction until there is a triangular fork in the path. Go left here, on to a cycle path and then immediately right on to a rough path to a squeeze stile in a small fence by the telegraph poles. Keeping at the crest of the slope, follow the path to the next line of fences.

13.   As you reach the end of the field, go through a squeeze stile which brings you out on to a grassy slope. Go straight ahead to the top of the mound, and look

for a kissing gate on the other side. This slope is quite steep so take care.

14. Through the kissing gate, you will find a path around a lake. Turn right and when you meet the junction, turn right again under the bridge and follow the wide path. As you go under the bridge the car park will come into view ahead of you. Go anti-clockwise around the lake to return to the car park and picnic area.

9. Swarkestone Pavilion Walk

Distance: 2.6 miles (Escape route reduces to 1.9 miles)

Description: This is an easy walk along canal paths and footpaths. It has many historical features, including Swarkestone Pavilion and Swarkestone Causeway and a possible picnic spot by the canal

Facilities: Refreshments and toilets at Crewe and Harpur pub and Swarkestone Garden Centre

Parking: Layby for around 10 spaces by Swarkestone Lock in Pingle Lane, DE73 6GN. Google Link VH52+87 Derby

Useful items: Duck food, walking stick, picnic if required.

Picnic Walks for Children around Derby and Derbyshire

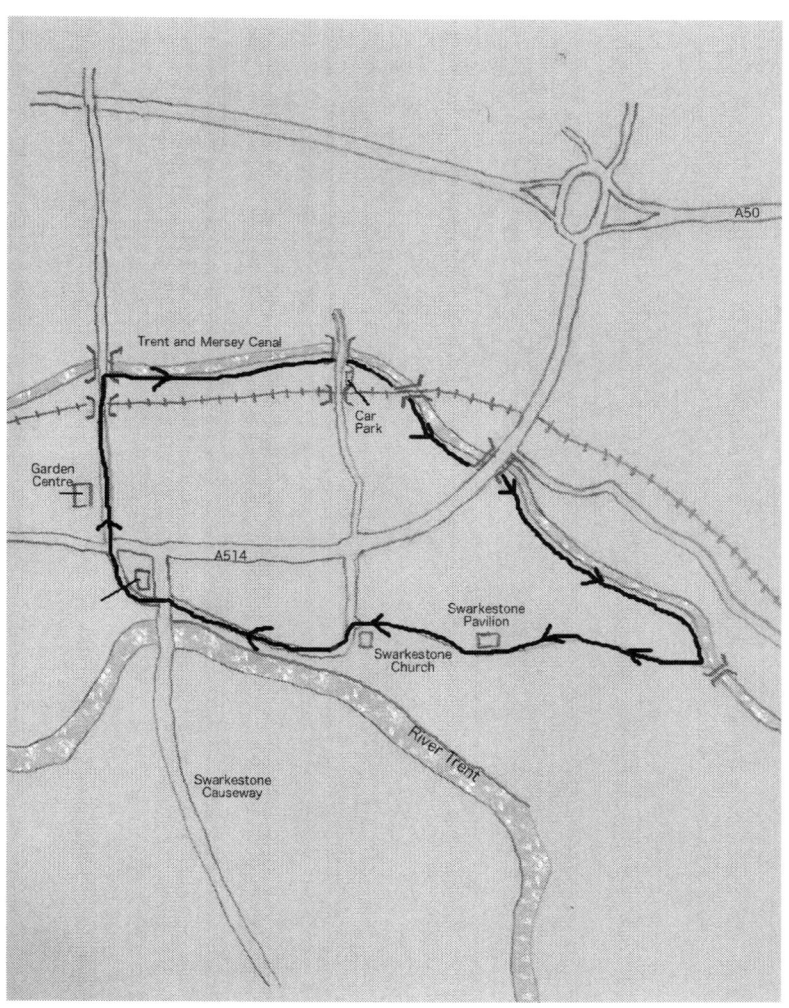

1. From the layby in Pingle Lane, walk towards the lock and turn right on to the canal path, with the canal on your left.

Swarkestone Lock is part of the Trent and Mersey Canal between the River Trent at Shardlow to Preston in Cheshire. The lock enables boats to go between the higher and lower stretches of the canal.

2. Walk along the canal to the third bridge, number 12, and take a path to the right just before the bridge, then immediately turn right again into a field.

There are lots of molehills along this walk. How many times can you spot them?

3. The path goes diagonally left across the field, towards a gap in the hedge with a yellow marker. Continue through the next field in the same direction to the left corner, to reach a gated concrete walkway across a ditch.

4. Through this gate, the path goes straight ahead to a kissing gate in the opposite hedge, then it follows the line of trees to the next gateway in the same direction.

5.   A stile will bring you into a small field adjacent to Swarkestone Pavilion.

> *Swarkestone Pavilion is now owned by the Landmark Trust and there is a flat large enough for two people. It is thought to have been a viewing point for competitions, possibly bowls or maybe even jousting. It belonged to Swarkestone Hall which was demolished in 1750 after it was damaged in the Civil War. Later it was acquired by the Harpur Crewe family of Calke Abbey. [Source: landmarktrustorg.uk]*

6.   Continue to a gateway ahead, across an access track and into the field with the boundary on your left, aiming for Swarkestone Church ahead. As you approach the church, follow the wall on the left to reach a stile in the corner.

7.   This stile brings you into an area beside the Swarkestone Church in Church Lane.

> **Escape Route:** *If you need a shorter walk, you can turn right on Church Lane, and then go across the main road into Pingle Lane.*

8.   To continue the walk, turn left on Church Lane. Ignore the footpath on your right – that footpath is an alternative route when the river floods the road.

9.   Follow the lane round to the right to walk alongside the River Trent.

At the end of this path, there is a Weeping Willow tree, and also a small Monkey Puzzle Tree – can you spot them?

10.   This path brings you to the main A514 opposite the Crewe and Harpur pub. Cross the road – TAKE CARE – BUSY ROAD.

On the left you can see Swarkestone Causeway built over the flood plain in the 13th century. Legend has it that it was commissioned by the two Bellamont sisters after they lost their fiancés in the swollen river. The ghosts of the sisters are said to haunt the bridge.

There was a minor battle here in the English Civil War and the Royalists (Charles I) were defeated by Cromwell's Parliamentarians in 1643. In 1745, it was the point at which Bonnie Prince Charlie turned back on his advance to London. [Source: Wikipedia]

11.   Go straight ahead into Woodshop Lane, and follow this around to the right, past the pretty

cottages, until you reach the main road. Cross Barrow Road into Lowes Lane – TAKE CARE – BUSY ROAD.

On the left along Lowes Lane, refreshments are available at Swarkestone Garden Centre, which has a café, children's area and toilets.

12. Further along Lowes Lane, you will cross a railway bridge and then there is a canal bridge. Just before the canal bridge, turn right down the steps to the canal path. Turn right along the canal path, with the water on your left.

13. About a quarter of a mile along the canal, the path widens out and there is a possible picnic spot with a seat available.

14. The path goes past a winter mooring area for barges and then to a former loading area for barges.

15. Continue along the towpath to return to Swarkestone Lock.

10. Carsington Reservoir (Pushchair, cycle and dog friendly)

Distance: 2.6 miles

Description: This is a fairly easy walk, firstly alongside the reservoir and then up a gentle slope along access roads, with interesting wood carvings and farm animals along the way.

Facilities: Toilets, kiosk and picnic area at the Millfields Car Park.

Parking: Millfields Picnic Area, Carsington Reservoir, DE6 3JL. Google Ref: 29W9+65 Ashbourne. Fees apply – walk takes approximately 2 hours.

Useful items: Duck food, binoculars, picnic if required, bird identifier.

Picnic Walks for Children around Derby and Derbyshire

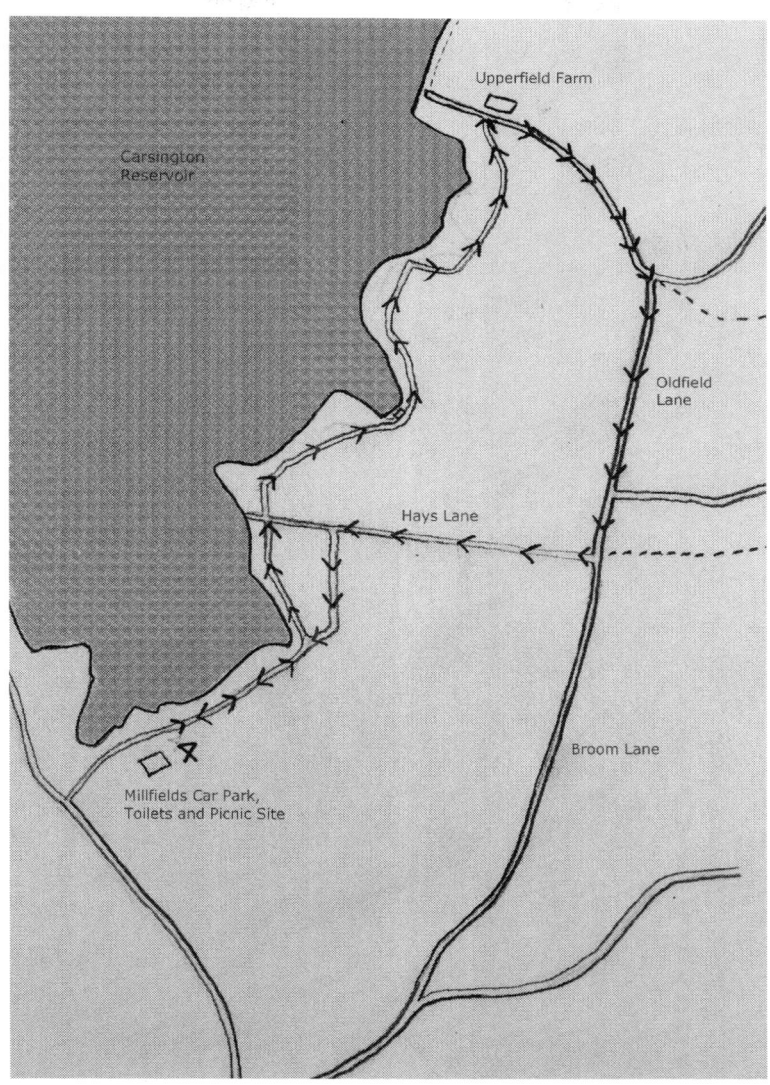

1.　　From the lower car park and picnic site, walk with the lake on your left, taking a path on your left to stay close to the lake, initially following the signs for the Sheepwash Car Park.

This is a good area to feed the birds. You will often see mallards in this area, with their colourful males and brown females.

2.　　Continue along the gravel path going slightly uphill. At the junction, keep left to stay close to the shoreline.

Activity: Can you count how many boats are sailing on the reservoir?

3.　　You will shortly see a stone hut on the left. Take the path left to look at the wood furniture in this hut.

4.　　From the stone hut, continue along the shoreline on a narrow path, passing an observation post, and turn left as you reach the wider path.

5.   Keep on this main path to reach a wood carving representing a pile of books.

Question: What words are written on the open book?

Answer: Out of the gloom the ghostly shape of a barn owl floated on to his outstretched arm.

6.   Continue on the main path along the lakeside until you reach a gate which leads on to a track by Upperfields Farm. Turn right uphill along this track, going past New Buildings Farm.

Activity: Look out for farm animals in the area on the right hand side.

7.   The track becomes a tarmac surface and reaches the junction of Bent Head Lane and Oldfield Lane. Turn right along Bent Head Lane which has views across the reservoir.

8.   Ignore the turn to Kirk Ireton and continue along Bent Head Lane, as it turns into Broom Lane.

Activity: Look out for the sheep in the fields. There are often lambs in the spring.

9.   After a short distance along Broom Lane, turn right down Hayes Lane, going past the Riddings Farm. Go through the gate at the bottom of the lane and then turn left to follow signs for Millfields Car Park. At the junction turn left and then immediately right at the signposts to return to the picnic site.

11. Tissington

Distance: 2.7 miles (Escape Route reduces to 1 mile)

Description: A fairly easy walk around Tissington village and across surrounding fields. There may be livestock in the fields.

Facilities: Toilets, food kiosk and picnic area at the Tissington Village and Trail Car Park. A café in Tissington Village.

Parking: Tissington Village and Trail Car Park, Darfield Lane, Tissington DE6 1RA. Google Ref: 3787+6J Ashbourne. Fees apply – the full walk takes approximately 2 hours. There are also free 2-hour spaces opposite Tissington Hall (start at point 6 from here).

Useful items: Duck food, picnic if required.

Picnic Walks for Children around Derby and Derbyshire

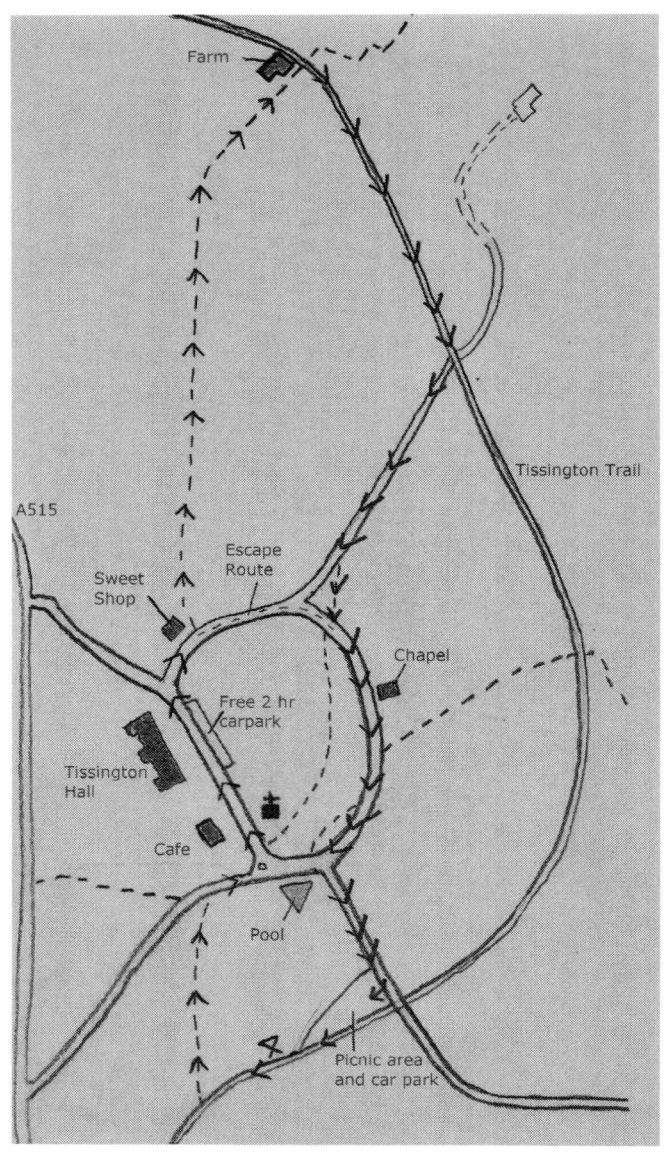

1. From the Tissington Trail car park, walk past the toilets, kiosk and picnic tables on to the Tissington Trail.

> *This is an area where you might see pheasants, and you may hear their croaking call in the woods around.*

2. When you go over a bridge, turn immediately right going down steps to a small gate in the fence next to a plaque stating Tissington Estate.

3. In the field, walk diagonally right to a gate in the far right hand corner, beside a wall, then with the wall on your right to a squeeze stile into another field. Keep the fence on your right, alongside poultry pens.

> *There are usually chickens and guinea fowl in these pens. The guinea fowl have very big black or white bodies with very small heads.*

4. Go to the gate in the far right corner and emerge into a lane beside a house built in 1891. On the main access road, turn right and walk into Tissington village.

5.	At the junction, turn left going past the church on your right, and there is also one of the famous wells on the right opposite the café.

Tissington is famous for its well-dressings which take place around May/June. The well-dressings have been the custom since 1349, after the village escaped the epidemic of the Black Death. [Source: Historic-uk.co.uk]

6.	Continue up Hall Cottages Lane, passing Tissington Hall on your left and parking bays on your right.

Tissington Hall is a Jacobean House which has been owned by the Fitzherbert family since the 1460s. The current building was built in 1609. [Source: tissinghall.co.uk]

7.	Walk up to the junction with Chapel Lane and turn right, passing Hands Well. You will soon arrive at the Edward and Vintage Shop which is an old-fashioned sweet shop. If you can resist the call

of the fudges and toffees, look for the footpath on the right hand side of the sweet shop, between two walls.

ESCAPE ROUTE: For the 1 mile walk, do not turn on to this footpath, but continue along Chapel Lane, following the road round to the right when it meets a country Lane. Then jump to point 14.

8. A small gate leads you into a field and the footpath follows the stone wall on your left to a small gate in the far wall. There are usually chickens in the enclosure on the left, and there may be livestock in the fields.

9. Continue through this field with the stone wall on your left to a step stile over the wall followed by a gate.

10. This next field is an example of medieval strip farming, with narrow mounds of land, and the path goes uphill, moving slightly diagonally right towards a marker post in the middle of the field, and then up to a stone post. A squeeze stile comes into view in the wall ahead.

> *Strip farming involved partitioning a field and renting out strips to villagers to grow their own crops.* [Source: historylearning.com]

11. Go through the squeeze stile and walk in the direction of the arrow on the stile to another squeeze stile ahead. In the next field the path goes slightly diagonally right uphill. As you reach the crest of the hill you can see the roof of farm buildings ahead. The

footpath goes through the left gateway into the farmyard. The farmer often provides a seating area, inviting walkers to rest a while.

12.	After passing through the farmyard, there is a sign pointing to the Tissington Trail. Follow the sign to take the path on the right which leads you down to the trail. Turn left on the trail and walk for approximately half a mile. As you pass under a bridge, look on the right for a signpost and this leads up steps to a gate on to a track.

Activity: As you go through the gate, can you spot a horseshoe embedded in the path?

13.	Turn left on the tarmac track, passing between farm buildings. Just after the farm buildings take a footpath on the left signposted for the Limestone Way, and go across the field to a gate in the far wall. Turn left down Chapel Lane.

14.	There is a Methodist Chapel on the left down this lane, which is sometimes open for viewing. As you continue down the lane you pass the butchers on the right and there is often a stall selling hand-made items on the left with an Honesty Box.

15.	To return to the start, keep left at the junction and the car park and picnic area will appear on your right. However you

may wish to go right for a short distance to feed the ducks in the village pond. There are also seats in this area where you could enjoy your picnic.

A Tissington Well dressing from June 2019

12. Long Eaton and Attenborough (Pushchair, cycle and dog friendly)

Distance: 3.3 miles

Description: This is an easy walk along riverside paths and footpaths. It starts at a picnic point with a playground and walks to Attenborough Nature Reserve. The return route is beside a railway with intermittent sightings of the Derby-Nottingham train.

Facilities: Toilets, café and picnic area at the Attenborough Nature Reserve. Playground at the Trent Meadows Picnic Site.

Parking: Car Park for around 10 cars at the Trent Meadows Picnic Site, Meadow Lane NG10 2FZ. This is reached from Acton Road, turning into Main Street by the Tappers Harker Pub. Google Link VPQW+XH Nottingham (Drive through the yellow goalposts at the entrance)

Useful items: Duck food, binoculars, picnic if required, bird identifier.

Picnic Walks for Children around Derby and Derbyshire

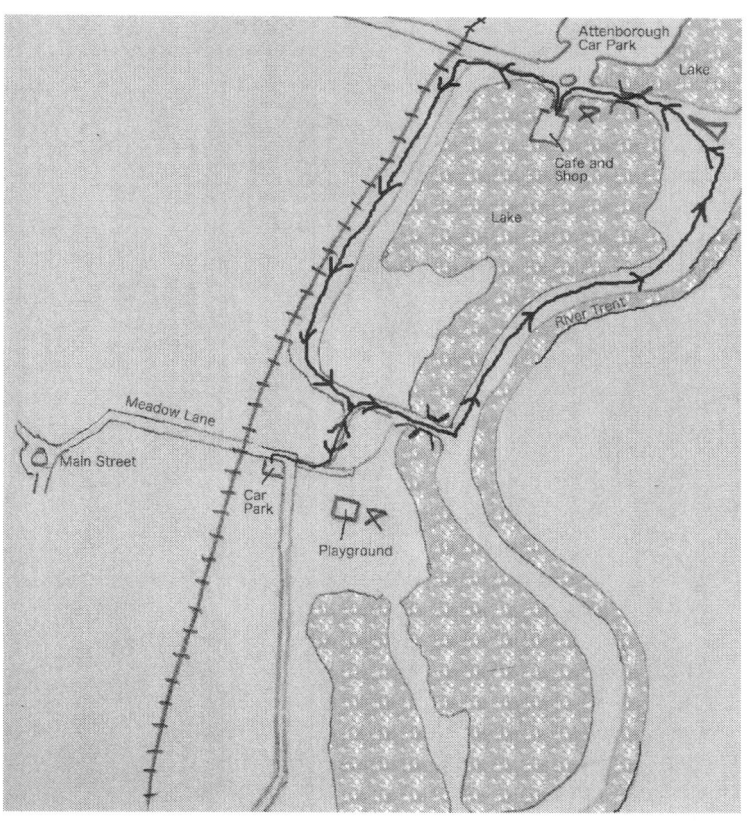

1. From the carpark, go through the squeeze stile by the gateway. Follow this path to reach the playground and picnic area.

2. Turn half left opposite the playground, going up the slope to the right of the Trent Meadows sign, until you reach a wide path at the end of the track.

[For the **pushchair route**, the lower left path is easier and goes to the same wide path.]

3. The upward path goes past a viewing seat looking out over the lake and then becomes narrower with denser bushes either side.

There are Hazel trees along this walk which will have catkins in the colder months. How many can you spot?

4. When you reach the wide path, turn right and follow this until you arrive at a bridge between two lakes. Go across the bridge and continue until you reach the river, where there is a seat on the right of the junction. Turn left along the river path and follow this for about a mile.

The lake on the left side of the path is home to many birds and you may see moorhens and coots. The moorhens are black with red beaks and the coots are black with white beaks.

Also along this path you may see teazels, which were once used in the textile industry as a natural comb for fabrics.

Activity: How many boats can you spot along the river?

5. Half way along the river path, you will come to a metal bridge. Just before the bridge, you can see a partly sunken boat in the lake to the left. The spire for Attenborough church is also visible on the left.

As you cross the metal bridge, look in the reeds as there is often a heron here searching for frogs and fish. You may also see a black cormorant (pictured left) as it sits on rocks in the lake to dry its wings.

6.   As the boat moorings on the river begin to thin, you will arrive at a gateway. Go through this to continue along the path, passing three buildings opposite a line of willow trees, and then another gateway just prior to a bridge with concrete walls. Immediately after the bridge there is a three-way junction. Turn left.

Look out for swans on the lakes around this area.

7.   As you leave the river behind, go over a bridge and you will arrive at the Attenborough car park. On the left is the picnic area and access to the café and toilets.

The café shop sells bags of duck food at reasonable prices. Also at the back of the café, there is a little sensory garden, leading to a hide where you can observe sand martins.

8.   From the line of rocks beside the car park entrance, take the footpath (Skylark trail) on the left through the trees. This path follows the line of the access road to reach a small car park through a squeeze stile. [**Pushchair users** may find the roadway preferable, up to the subsidiary carpark.]

9. Go through the subsidiary carpark to a green gate leading to the track beside the railway line, marked the skylark trail. The track immediately curves left to follow the railway line.

Activity: Count how many trains pass as you walk.

10. Follow this road up to the sailing club, and keeping on the wide path, cross a bridge labeled 39T.

> *Among the animals in the fields on the left, you can sometimes see black sheep and also alpacas.*

11. At the end of the fields, where there is a large pylon, the path moves away from the railway and goes through a copse beside Barton Wood nature reserve. As you leave the woodland, the path makes a sharp left turn and goes under the electricity wires.

12. Shortly after going under the wires, ignore the first path on the right, and then take the next path on the right beside a seat. This leads back to the picnic tables and playground. Turn right for the car park.

13. Sutton Bonington and the Zouch Cut

Distance: 4.3 miles (Escape Route to avoid weir reduces to 2.8 miles)

Description: This is an easy walk along riverside paths and footpaths. **Please note that there is deep water and a weir so please keep children safe. The weir is very noisy and may be a little scary.**

Facilities: Picnic places along the route. Playground at the Sutton Bonington car park. Refreshments available at the Rose and Crown, Zouch or the Kings Head, Sutton Bonington.

Parking: Bottle Bank/Playing Fields car park on Main Street, Sutton Bonington LE12 5PF (Google Link RPCX+F3 Loughborough)

Useful items: Duck food, binoculars, picnic if required.

Picnic Walks for Children around Derby and Derbyshire

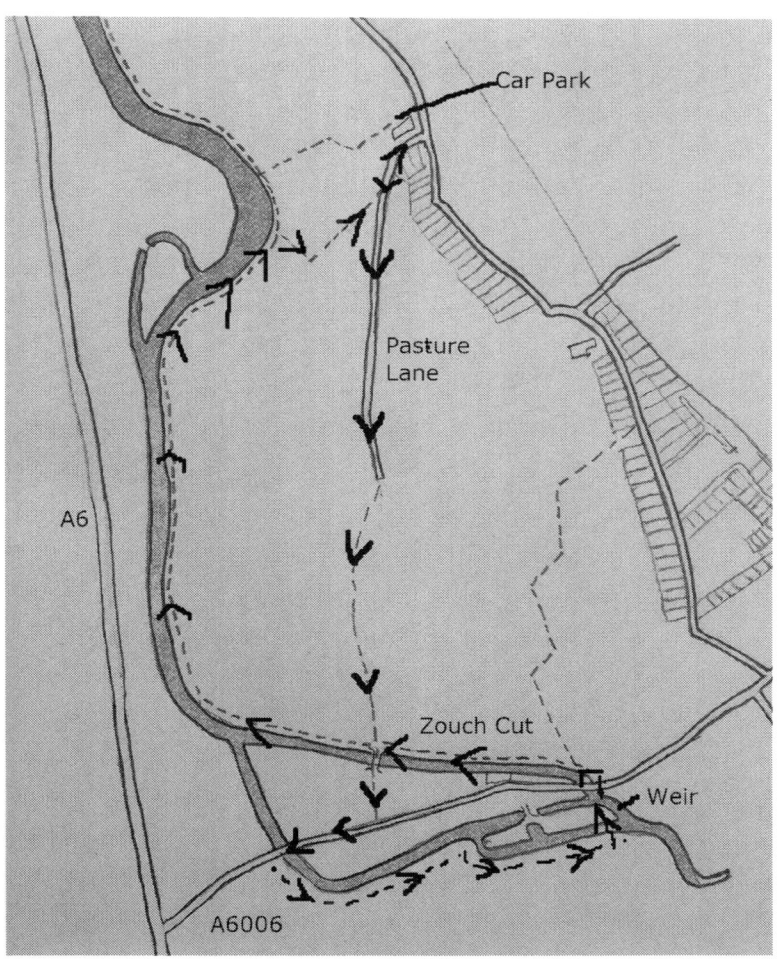

1.   From the carpark, walk past the playground towards the road, and turn right along the pavement, going past the Kings Head pub. Shortly after the pub, turn right into Pasture Lane.

2.   Walk to the end of the houses and then follow a bridle path sign along a farm track. Ignore the footpath on the right and continue along the track, going past a bench and the entrance to Diamond Wood, until you reach a gate with a footpath sign.

3.   Go through the gate and continue in the same direction along the farm track across two fields. At the end of the second field veer left to leave the track and go to the left of a short hedge and then a longer

hedge. Keeping the longer hedge on your right, go to the end of the field to reach a bridge over a canal.

4.   ESCAPE ROUTE: This is the point where you can opt for the shorter walk to omit the weir, which is spectacular but noisy. For the shorter route, turn right before the bridge and jump to paragraph 12.

5.   For the longer walk, go straight across the bridge. Go through the bridge gate and carry on in the same direction straight across the field to reach a gate to the main road. **BUSY ROAD - PLEASE TAKE CARE.**

6.   Turn right along the road and continue until you go over the river bridge. Cross the road carefully to a footpath at the side of the bridge. Follow this footpath going over two stiles down a slope and turn immediately left, to reach a further stile by a gate just under the electricity wires by the pylon.

7.   Keep on this path with the river on your left along a track, going over another stile by a gate into a field. There is a further gate ahead, and adjacent is an unusual corner stile on the left. Return to the track to keep following the river as it curls round to the right and then to the left. There is another gateway with a stile to the left here.

8. At the next gateway with the warning signs, the footpath continues into this section and leads to the weir. As you get close to the weir, there is a corrugated shed on the left and then a  copse. Walk between the shed and the copse to reach a bridge over the weir.

9. After the first bridge, follow the path right and then left to go over a second bridge leading to Turnpike Island, which has been set up as a picnic site in a precarious position.

10. Continue across the final bridge. On the left is a house on the side of the river with two pixies on the patio.

Activity: Can you spot the statue of a cow in the garden of the house beside the weir?

11. The path leads up to the main road, close to the Rose and Crown pub. TAKE CARE – BUSY ROAD. Cross the road and turn right to find a footpath sign on the left just over the bridge. This leads back to the canal. Follow this track around to the left, ignoring footpath signs on the right into the field. Walk alongside the canal, passing the rear of the Rose and Crown pub, until you reach the bridge again.

This a possible place to feed the ducks.

12. From the bridge, walk with canal on your left towards the lock.

This section is known as the Zouch Cut, which allows boats to get around the weirs safely. The lock ahead is to allow boats to adjust to the level of the canal beyond.

Activity: How many boats can you count on the canal and river?

13. There is a gate ahead with a stile. The canal meets the River Soar at this point and the path follows the river round to the right. Keep on the river path to go through 3 kissing gates to reach Diamond Wood.

> *This wood is maintained by the University of Nottingham and there are paths which can be explored, as well as seats which would make a possible picnic spot. There is an information plaque which gives details of flora and fauna.*

14. Leave Diamond Wood by a further kissing gate and continue with the river on your left.

15, At the next kissing gate, the path goes close to the river to the left of a copse. KEEP CHILDREN SAFE BY THE WATER.

16. Immediately after going through the gate, there is a low wall and just after the corner, there is a footpath sign by the wall. Climb over the wall at this point to follow the footpath sign to Sutton Bonington over a plank bridge and through a kissing gate into a field.

17. Walk along the side of the field with the hedge and brook on your left, to reach a gateway and footpath sign also on your left just before the corner of the field.

18.   Turn left here through the kissing gate and go along a fenced path between paddocks, usually containing horses.

19.   This path leads to another kissing gate over a plank bridge. Turn left here into Pasture Lane and walk to the main road.

20.   At the main road, turn left to go past the Kings Head and then left past the playground and into the carpark.

14. Snelston and the River Dove

Distance: 4.4 m

Description: A fairly easy walk on canal and river paths, fields and quiet lanes.

Facilities: A quirky stile, pretty villages and a former corn mill. Farm animals and pheasants often seen in surrounding fields. Picnic opportunity on the green by the Ashbourne Shrovetide Football goal.

Parking: On-road parking beside Snelston Church in Church Road, Snelston DE6 2EP. Google Ref: X6PH+VX Ashbourne

Useful items: Picnic if required.

Picnic Walks for Children around Derby and Derbyshire

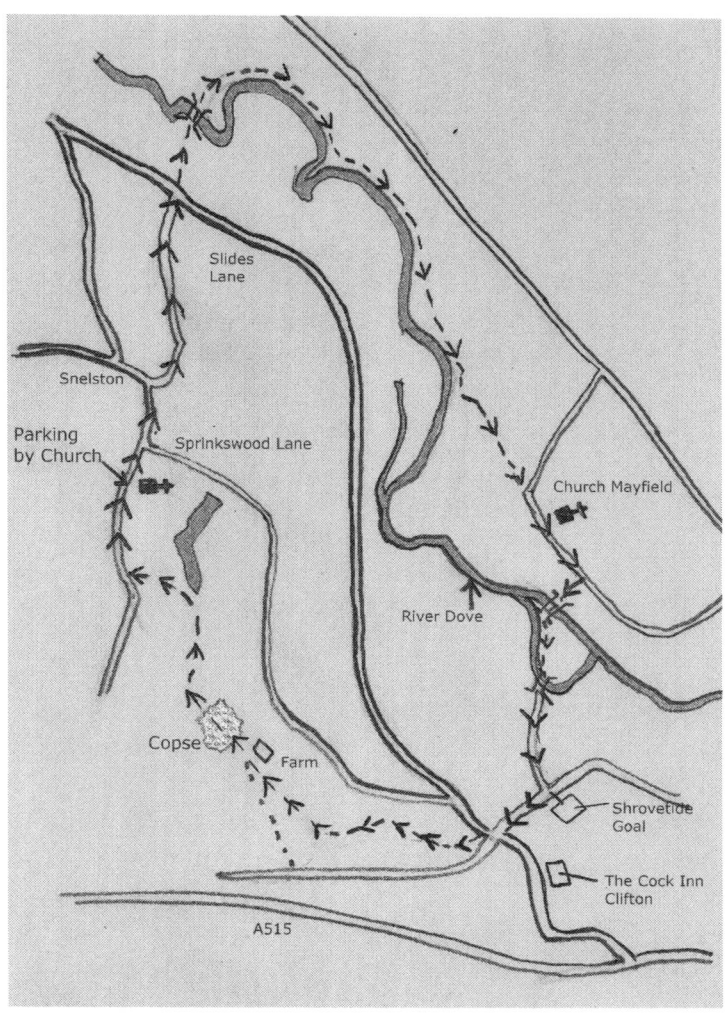

1. With your back to the church, turn right along Church Road. Continue on this road, crossing Sprinkswood Lane, until you reach the junction in Snelston beside the memorial obelisk. Turn right and follow the road around the bend for roughly half a mile.

2. At the T-junction, cross the road carefully, following the footpath sign through a gateway to the left of a farm shed. Follow the track through the field gate to reach Toadhole Footbridge over the River Dove.

Snelston village was designated a model village, after Squire John Harrison had it remodeled in 1847. The Hall was demolished in 1951 and the current Snelston Hall was created from the former stable block. [Source: Snelston.com]

3. From the bridge, walk across the field diagonally right to rejoin the river at the far bend. Follow the river round to the right, going through two stiles. The path leaves the river briefly to rejoin at the next bend, with a stile beside two trees next to a gateway.

4. The footpath forks at this gateway. Take the right fork to go straight on, walking in the general direction of the river to another gateway and stile.

5. As you go through the next gateway and stile, the church of Church Mayfield comes into view, and this gives a guide for your general direction. The next stile is tucked in the right-hand corner – a little gate leading to a plank bridge and a second gate.

6. Veer left as you enter the next field, and with the boundary on your right follow it round to the next gateway and stile. Head towards the church with the boundary on your right to a stile in the corner, taking you on to a roadway. Turn right and follow the road into Church Mayfield.

7. Proceed past the church until there is a row of terraced houses on your left. Opposite No. 6 turn right to follow a footpath sign next to a plaque, which gives details of the buildings around and how they related to the Corn Mill.

8. Follow this footpath round the bend until you reach a metal bridge over the mill race. Turn left at the end of the bridge and then veer right through the mill buildings, emerging on to the access road.

9. Turn right along the access road to rejoin the river at the bridge. Walk along the road for a quarter of a mile to a T-junction. The green on the opposite side of the road provides a picnic area.

A plaque on the green explains that this is the down'ards goal for the Shrovetide football game, and the goalpost can be seen from the small footbridge across the stream at the rear of the green.

10. From the green, turn left, watching out for any traffic. As you reach the crossroads at Clifton, turn right.

The Cock Inn, Clifton, is a few hundred yards up the road to the left if you require refreshments at this point.

11. Immediately after turning right at the crossroads, cross the road carefully to a footpath sign leading into a field. In the field, the path veers upwards to the right across the middle of the field, towards two large trees by a gap in the hedge. Go up the steps and through a squeeze stile into another field.

12. Keeping in the same direction, go straight up the hill towards a group of trees at the top.

This group of trees is known as Margery Bower, a round burial mound thought to be from the Bronze Age. It is also said to be the site of Cromwell's cannons in 1645 as he attacked retreating Royalists after the Battle of Naseby. [Source: Derbyshireuk.net]

13.   Slightly to the right and behind the Bower there is a gateway leading to a farm track. Follow this track as it winds between the trees to emerge into a narrow field just before the farmyard.

14.   Veer left to walk along the centre of this field, with a large farm building on your right. Turn diagonally right as you pass the farm buildings and go towards the line of fencing up the slope ahead. The stile is in the corner at the far right-hand end of the fence, where it meets a gateway.

15.   Go left over the stile into a field and turn sharp right to follow the fence line towards a small wood.

16.   Go through the small gate into the wood.

You have now entered Snelston Hall grounds and there are often pheasants in this area. Can you spot any? The male is colourful with long tail feathers and a red head, whereas the female is mainly brown. Also listen out for woodpeckers in this wood.

17. Follow the path through the wood to a fence on the other side.

Activity: Can you work out how to get through the fence? It incorporates a very clever stile. (See the photo overleaf if you need a clue.)

18. The path goes straight ahead down the field towards a stile and gate in the fence at the bottom. There are often sheep in this field, and to the right, you can see a lake with Snelston Hall beyond.

As you walk down the hill, there is a copse of Monkey Puzzle trees on your right, which are part of 80 trees planted on the orders of Squire John Harrison in the middle of the 19th Century.

19. From the gateway turn diagonally right, and gradually move higher up the slope as you walk along the centre of the field. As the corner of the top fence comes into view, just before a few trees in a line across the field and along a ditch, turn sharp left towards a gateway. Go through the gateway to the

road, and turn right. Watch out for any cars along this road.

20. As you follow the road round to the right, the church and the parking space come into view. You will pass the gatehouse for Snelston Hall just before you return to the start point.

Did you work out how to get through the fence?

15. Thorpe, Mapleton and the River Dove

Distance: 4.4 miles

Description: Some rough paths and hilly terrain combined with riverside paths and the Tissington Trail.

Facilities: Picnic Area, a giraffe! and a public house en route

Parking: Thorpe Station Car Park, off Narlows Lane, DE6 2AT. Google Ref: 26XW+X9 Ashbourne. This is half a mile from the main Narlows Lane carpark, and is down a track beside the triangle.

Useful items: Picnic if required, hiking boots, a walking stick may be helpful.

Picnic Walks for Children around Derby and Derbyshire

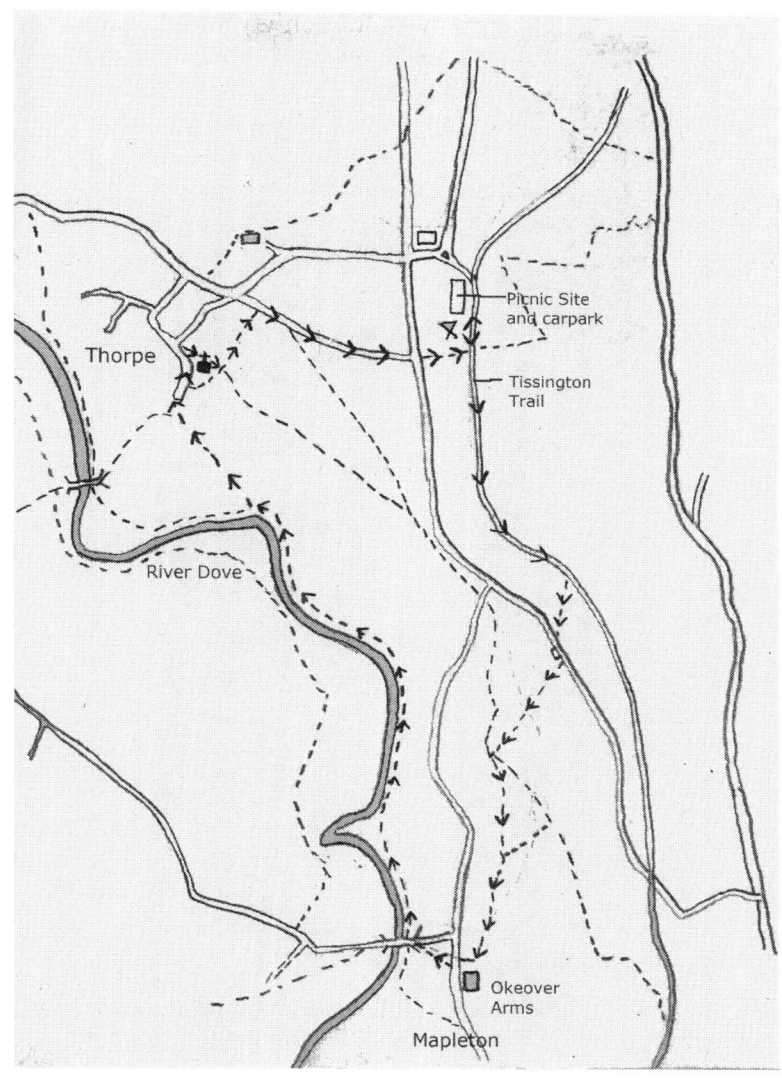

1.   From the picnic area in Thorpe Station car park, turn right on the Tissington Trail and walk for approximately ¾ mile, past footpath signs and over a wooden bridge, until you see a footpath on the right between two trees leading to a kissing gate.

2.   The kissing gate will bring you into a field and the footpath goes straight ahead up a slope to the right of a clump of trees, to a small gate in the top level with the tree-line.

3.   In the next field, the path goes diagonally left towards a building. The gate-stile is to the right of the building and takes you on to a road.

4.   Walk left along the road a short way to find a footpath sign on the left, pointing to a squeeze stile on the right. Go right here into the drive of a house keeping along the fence on the left, to a gated

footpath which leads past a newly built house on the left.

5.   Ignore the gate on the right and take the gate to the left of this straight ahead and into a small field. Keeping the fence on your right, head for a stile in the corner on the right-hand side. Over this rickety stile, veer diagonally right across the field to reach a stile in the corner where the square copse meets the boundary. This stile goes over a plank bridge into a field – turn right in this field heading for a gate in the right corner.

6.   Just after this gate, turn sharp left through another gate which takes you into a small wood. Follow this path through the woodland, to emerge through a small gate into a field.

7.   Go diagonally right towards the fence and then walk with the fence on your right-hand side. The village of Mapleton comes into view in front to your right, and this gives the general direction to aim for.

8.   At the end of the fence line, go through a small gate and walk diagonally right down the hill. The path goes towards the lower end of a line of trees. Walk to a stile hidden in the trees between the two gates.

9.   Follow the arrow on the stile, keeping the hedge on your right-hand side and walk through the field, which often has sheep grazing. Look out for a short signpost halfway along the edge of the field indicating

two footpaths, and at that point go diagonally right to the corner of the field.

10. As you near the boundary on the right hand side, you can see a small Methodist chapel and graveyard through the trees. Follow the boundary past the churchyard and the yard of the Okeover Arms until you see a footpath on the right leading to the road.

11. Turn right to the Okeover Arms where refreshment is usually available. Opposite the Okeover Arms there is a footpath sign "Public Footpath to Dovedale" which takes you into a field. Walk diagonally right, skirting the corner of a property to emerge on the road just to the right of a bridge over the River Dove.

12. Walk carefully across the road to a little gate into a field and follow the line of the river to a stile in the left-hand corner of the next boundary hedge.

13. Walk alongside the river to go over a stile in the next hedge under the telegraph poles.

From this path, you can see the peak of Thorpe Cloud in the distance.

14. Go through a squeeze stile into the next field. There is a sharp bend in the river here and the path goes diagonally right across the field to meet the river again in the corner. Go through a gap in the hedge and keep the river on your left.

15. Go through a gap in the trees to the next stile, which is a plank bridge across a brook.

Activity: Can you spot a giraffe in the trees on the right?

16. Take care as the path goes very close to the river along the next stretch of path. Go through a squeeze stile and then over a three plank bridge crossing another stream, to follow a fenced-in path, still with the river on your left.

This is an area where you might see pheasants, and there are often swans and mallards along the river.

17. Continue along the fenced-in path through 3 boundaries, until a kissing gate brings you into a field. Walk straight ahead to follow the river. In the corner of this field, there is a gateway with a small gate at the side of it and a plank bridge, and immediately after

this bridge, turn sharp right along a footpath signposted for Thorpe.

> *Wild garlic grows all around this woodland in the spring and summer and you may be surrounded by the aroma.*

18. Keep on the main path going up the hill, ignoring any side paths, until you reach a small gate into a field. Go slightly diagonally right up this field towards the left hand side of the fence in front of a property. Go through a gate on the corner in the middle of the field, following the track to the left and then on to a farm track, turning right to go through a gate and past the houses.

19. At St Leonard's Church, go through the gate into the churchyard and walk around the church on the right side.

> *The grooves on the side of the church doorway are arrow-sharpening marks made during the reign of Edward III in the 14th century, when men were required to practice. The butts were at the bottom of the churchyard and took place after Sunday service. [Source: Derbyshireheritage.co.uk]*

Question: **There is a sundial to the right of the church door. Why is it so high?**

Answer: **It is thought that this**

was used by horse-riders. As the sundial is not perfectly calibrated, it is likely that it was moved to its current position from elsewhere. [Source: derbyshireheritage.co.uk]

20.   Follow the path around the church to the left, down into a lower graveyard, and then left through a gate to a driveway. Turn right onto the driveway down a slope and as it meets another path, turn sharp left.

21.   Walking with the wall on your right, continue to go over a small bridge over the stream. Go straight ahead roughly following the stream and go over another wooden bridge to a grassy area leading to a lane. Turn right to go up the steep lane.

22.   Go past Broadlow Ash Farm and along the track to reach the main road. Carefully cross the main road to a footpath opposite through a small gate. Walk with the boundary on your left to another small gate into a larger field.

23.   Walk straight ahead down the hill to a kissing gate leading to the Tissington Trail. Turn left and the picnic area and carpark will shortly come into view.

16. Shardlow Canal and Church Wilne

Distance: 4.6 miles (Escape Routes provide shorter walks of half a mile, 3.2 and 4 miles)

Description: A fairly easy walk on canal and river paths, fields and quiet lanes. There are 4 possible routes to provide walks for children of all ages. There is a canal lock to cross by a narrow footbridge and also deep water close to some paths, so please keep children safe.

Facilities: Picnic areas, playground, bird sanctuary, boats, former inland port (see plaque in car park for details of buildings).

Parking: Wilne Lane Car Park, Shardlow, DE72 2HG. Google Ref VM95+VX Derby

Useful items: Duck food, binoculars, picnic if required, bird book.

Picnic Walks for Children around Derby and Derbyshire

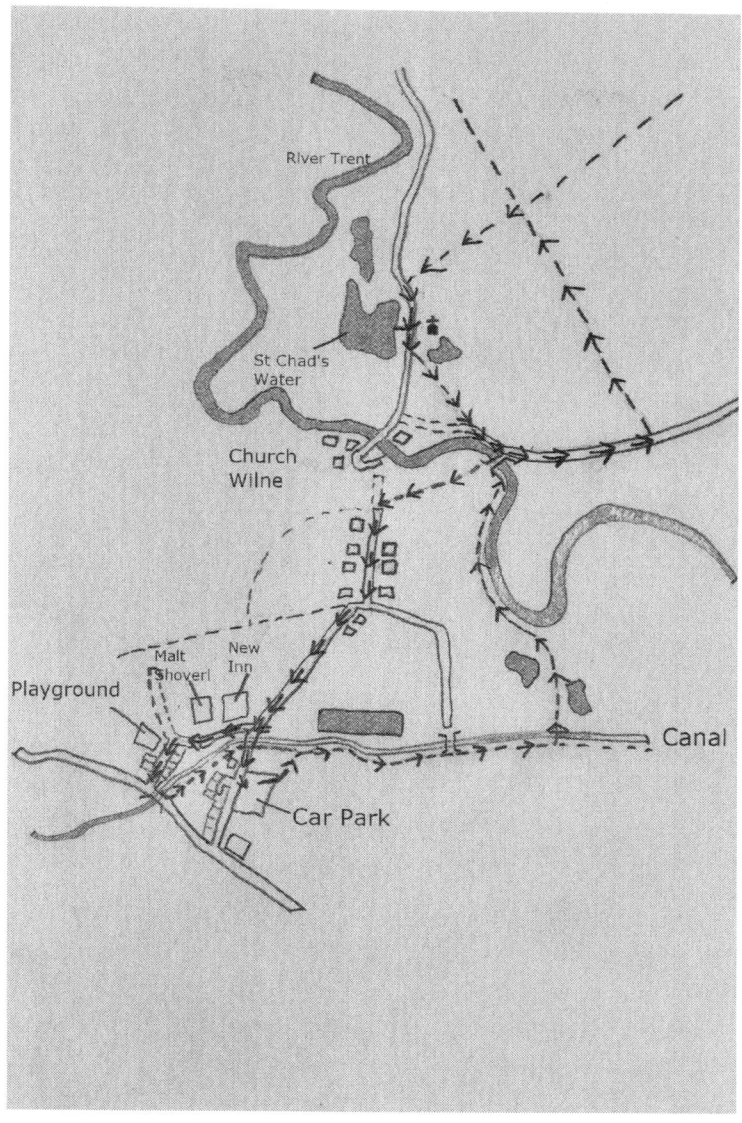

1.   For the shorter ½ mile route which goes round the former inland port, return to Wilne Lane and turn right. Walk to the canal and cross the bridge, turning left along the road in front of the New Inn pub. Then follow the directions from point 17.

2.   For the longer routes, go to the rear of the car park and go through the squeeze stile on to a tree—lined pathway.

3.   The path curves round to cross a wider path. Veer right here and then immediately left along the crest of a grassy bank towards the canal. Turn right along the canal bank and walk for a quarter of a mile, to go under Bridge No. 1.

Activity: There are many barges resident along the canal. Can you read their names?

4.   Continue along the canal for another quarter of a mile to a lock, with a narrow bridge across. Cross the canal on this bridge. TAKE CARE – DEEP WATER.

5. Veering left, cross a further bridge and follow the path beside the water race. Go over the stile and into a field, walking along the boundary with the hedge on your right.

Then go across a second stile by a pond into a further field. The path goes straight ahead across the centre of the field towards a fallen tree trunk that resembles an archway.

6. Go over a stile to turn left along the river path. Go over another stile into a field, and continue along the river bank, going through an open boundary hedge, over another stile to aim for the bridge across the river.

> ESCAPE ROUTE: *If you wish to do the 3.2 mile route, turn 90 degrees left at the bridge, to take a footpath across the field heading for the house on the far side, and jump to point 14.*

7. For the longer route, go right over the bridge and turn left on the riverside path up to the road. Turn right along the road, watching out for the occasional car.

8. Walk along the road for approximately a third of a mile to find a public footpath, next to a bridle path, on the left. Cross the stile into the field, and walk along the boundary keeping the hedge on your left, to a further stile in the far left corner.

Many gorse bushes grow in this area, sporting yellow flowers in the spring. Can you spot these?

9. Walk up the slope and follow the path along the top of the grassy embankment, with the fence on your right.

Along this path, you can see the church tower of Church Wilne on the left. You will get a closer look at this shortly.

10. At the end of the path, turn left along a rough bridle path, ignoring footpath signs on your right. Walk to the end of this path, going through a gate and then up to the road. Turn left along the road.

Activity: Look out for signs of horses along this path – can you see the hoofprints? There are often horses in the fields on the right.

11. Walk along the road for about a quarter of a mile. Just before the church there is an entrance on the right to St. Chad's Water. This is an excellent picnic spot and an opportunity to feed the birds.

Activity: Check out the plaques on the fence on the left just before the church. Some of these are memorials to people killed in the First World War, and there are also some giving an amusing history of Church Wilne.

12. Return to the road from St Chad's Water and turn right to go past the church and find a footpath sign on the left partly hidden in the trees. Turn left through the open gateway into the copse which is mainly made up of pussy willow trees. The path is often covered by catkins from the trees in the spring.

13. The path goes through another gateway into an agricultural field. Go straight across this field to a similar gateway leading to the road. Turn left along the road and walk for around a quarter of a mile, looking for a footpath on the right. Follow the sign to a river path which returns to the river bridge. Cross the bridge and continue in the same direction across

the field, heading towards a house on the far side of the field.

14. As you get close to the house, head for the gateway on a wide farm track. Turn left to go over a stile at the side of the left gateway. Walk along the road (Wilne Lane) for approximately half a mile to reach the canal bridge.

15. ESCAPE ROUTE: You can continue straight over the bridge and walk a short way down Wilne Lane to the car park on the left.

16. To continue to a playground and picnic area, turn to the right before the bridge to pass the New Inn and the Malt Shovel, where refreshments can be purchased.

This area was an important inland port in the 18th and early 19th centuries and many of the houses have been converted from warehouses. Large cargo ships would have been loading and unloading at this port, and these were able to reach the Humber estuary from Shardlow.

17. The road bends to the left and at the end of this cul-de-sac, there is an alley on the right. This brings you to another cul-de-sac and there is a

playground and picnic area on the right. (Shardlow Children's Play Area)

18. From the picnic area, turn right along the road. Walk to the end of the road and turn left on to main road. TAKE CARE – BUSY ROAD.

19. Walk over the bridge and immediately turn left to go on to the towpath along the canal.

Activity: This is good place to feed the ducks. You can often see mallards and swans along this stretch.

20. Follow the towpath until you can see the New Inn on the opposite side of the canal and a bridge ahead. Go up the steps beside the bridge and turn right into Wilne Lane. The car park is a short way along on the left hand side.

Copyright © 2021 Hazel Glover

All Rights Reserved

KDP ISBN: 9798743615124
Independently Published
April 2021

Printed in Great Britain
by Amazon